IRISH SAINTS

First published in 1999 by
Mercier Press
PO Box 5 5 French Church St Cork
Tel: (021) 275040; Fax: (021) 274969; e.mail: books@mercier.ie
16 Hume Street Dublin 2
Tel: (01) 661 5299; Fax: (01) 661 8583; e.mail: books@marino.ie

Trade enquiries to CMD Distribution 55A Spruce Avenue
Stillorgan Industrial Park Blackrock County Dublin
Tel: (01) 294 2556; Fax: (01) 294 2564
e-mail: cmd@columba.ie

ISBN 1 85635 253 6
10 9 8 7 6 5 4 3 2 1

Cover photograph courtesy of Paul Larmour
Printed in Ireland by ColourBooks Baldoyle Dublin 13

IRISH SAINTS

PEG COGHLAN

MERCIER PRESS

INTRODUCTION

Ireland, as all her schoolchildren used to learn, was known in the golden age of monasticism as *Isola sanctorum doctorumque* – the 'isle of saints and scholars'. There were indeed many *sancti* and many *docti* at that time, and several even managed to be both. The martyrologies list numerous saints, some with well-documented lives, others known only nominally. At least 350 Colmáns, twenty Ultáns, twenty-two Senans, thirty-seven Moluas and several Finnians and Ciaráns are listed. Most have local reputations, and miraculous powers have been assigned to the broken chancels and crosses, the holy wells and the round towers that are their memorials. The great saints like Patrick, Brigid and Colum Cille have enough wonder tales associated with them to fill books. Indeed such books do exist, but they cannot bear scrutiny either by cleric or historian. The facts as we can discern them are wonderful enough. The proliferation of Irish saints is all the more miraculous in that only three were formally canonised – St Malachy, St Laurence O'Toole and St Oliver Plunkett – the latter having languished as 'Blessed' from 1920 until 1975. The only other saint for whom the process of beatification has been initiated is Venerable Matt Talbot.

Even before St Patrick came, Christians in Ireland were praising God and revelling in the world he had created. They celebrated the seasons' changes and the great variety of flora and fauna that their beloved island boasted. So, even though the monasteries founded by the early saints were noted for the severity of their rules and the austerity of the lives that their monks led, some found that the regime was too easy and imposed even greater mortifications upon themselves for the greater glory of God. The phrase used by the old hagiographers was *bán-martra* – 'bloodless martyrdom' – by which a person renounces everything he loves for God. These ascetics chose to exile themselves in lonely hermitages on mountains, on islands in remote lakes or offshore, or in isolated places like Sceilg Mhichíl off the coast of County Kerry. The greatest, most heartbreaking exile was to go as a *peregrinus* – an itinerant missionary – to preach Christ to the barbarian and heretic in the brutish Europe of the Dark Ages.

The brief stories of the holy men and women related in this book are as authentic as modern scholarship can render them. Most belong to the period 400-800 AD when Christianity was being rooted and re-rooted in Western Europe, but the inclusion of some moderns shows that there are still many Irish saints about – all covered by the blanket Feast of All the Saints of Ireland, which is solemnised each year on 6 November.

A

Abbán (fifth century) was said to be a contemporary of St Patrick* and a nephew of St Ibar*. A member of one of the four chief families of Leinster, Abbán founded the monasteries of Killabban near Laois and Moyarney near New Ross in that province. He is sometimes associated with a second-century saint called Abben, who is thought to be the founder of the Berkshire town of Abingdon. Abbán's feast day is 16 March.

Adamnán of Iona (624-704), the son of Ronan and Ronnat, was born in Raphoe and educated locally. He went to Iona in 652 and became the ninth abbot there in 679. In 686 he visited a former pupil, Aldfrid, king of Northumbria, to obtain the release of sixty Irish captives and got to know the monks of Jarrow and Wearmouth. Probably as a result, he was the foremost Columban monk to accept the rulings about church matters laid down at the Synod of Whitby in 664, but he failed to persuade the monks of his own abbey to follow them. He returned to Ireland with the mission of reconciling the Celtic and Roman churches, and at the synod at Birr in 697, he sponsored the *Cáin Adamnáin*, a codex of laws for the protection of religious, women and children, especially in time of war. In the decade after 688 he wrote *Vita Columbae*, the life of his second cousin Colum Cille*, the founder of Iona, and *De Locis Sanctis,* an account of the holy places of Palestine taken down from the Frankish Bishop Arculf. Adamnán died in Iona having founded several 'Roman' monasteries in Ireland, including one near his birthplace. The modern form of his name is Eunan and his feast day is 23 September.

Adamnán (d. 680) was a Irish pilgrim who joined the Benedictine monastery of Coldingham, near Berwick on the Scottish border. The place had been founded by St Ebba, the sister of the kings of Northumbria, as a double monastery. The Irishman was noted for his extreme fasts and vigils. His feast day is 31 January.

Aidan aka Maedoc (d. 626) was a native of Connacht and one of the most significant students of St David at his monastery of Menevia in Wales. He established a monastery at Ferns in County Wexford and became the first bishop of the diocese. His feast day is 31 January.

Aidan of Lindisfarne (d. 651) was an Irish monk of Iona, believed to have been educated at St Senan*'s monastery at Scattery Island in the Shannon estuary. He was sent at the request of St Oswald, king of Northumbria, to evangelise the north of England. He established a community on the tidal Holy Island at Lindisfarne opposite Bamburgh, the residence of the king, in 635 and spent the next fifteen years preaching and ordaining a native clergy. His diocese eventually stretched from the Forth to the Humber and was home to many churches and monasteries, including the famous Melrose near Galashiels in the Scottish border country. In his time both Christian kings of Northumbria, Oswald and Oswin, venerated since as saints, were murdered and Aidan's life was often in danger. He is usually represented in art with a stag, a reference to the legend that he rendered invisible a deer which was being hunted. His biographer was the Venerable Bede (673-735) and his feast day is 31 August.

Mary Aikenhead (1787-1858), founder of the Irish Sisters of Charity, was the daughter of a Protestant doctor from Cork who had married a Catholic, Mary Stackpole. For the first six years of her life, she was fostered by a Catholic family called O'Rourke and brought up as a Protestant, but she became a Catholic after her father's deathbed conversion. She worked among the poor in Cork and was soon in correspondence with Dr Murray, Archbishop of Dublin, about joining an order of sisters who could do the work more effectively. As it turned out, she was the only member of the order and after training in a convent in York, she opened her first house in North William Street, Dublin, with one other sister, Alicia Walsh. By the time of her death after years of invalidism, the order had established ten houses and founded St Vincent's Hospital. Since then, the sisters have established communities throughout the world and were pioneers in the care of convicts in penal Australia. The decree for the introduction of the cause for her beatification was initiated in 1921 by Benedict XV.

Ailbe aka Ailbhe (d. 527) is venerated as a pre-Patrician Irish bishop. He was consecrated in Rome and founded the diocese of Emly, west of Cashel. It was there that he met St Patrick* and acknowledged him as his religious superior. Among the wonder tales associated with his early life is a story that as the child of a maidservant Ailbe was exposed but rescued and reared by wolves. He encouraged St Enda* to found the earliest Irish monastic settlement on Inishmore in the Aran Islands. His feast day is 12 September.

Algise aka Adalgis (d. *c.* 686) was an Irish monk, one of the disciples of St Fursa*, and he evangelised the area round Arras and Laon in northeast France. The village of St Algis in Picardy grew up from a small monastery founded by the saint in the centre of the forest of Thiq'erarche. His feast day is 2 June.

Alto (d. 760) was an Irish monk who settled as a hermit around 743 in a wood near the modern Augsburg in Germany. The town of Altenmünster (Alto's abbey) originated from his hermitage. His feast day is 9 February.

Aodh aka Aedh Mac Bricc, Aidus (sixth century), may have come from Meath but is associated with Donegal, where there is an oratory with his name on Slieve League. He studied with St Illadan of Rathlihen, County Offaly and founded the church of Rathugh in County Westmeath. His feast day is 10 November.

Assic aka Asicus (d. *c.* 490) was an early disciple of St Patrick* and founded an establishment at Elphin in Roscommon. He was made bishop of the diocese of that name and is its patron. A coppersmith by trade, he made patens and shrines for the early Church. His feast day is 27 April.

Attracta aka Athrachta (fifth century) was a contemporary of St Patrick*. Born in Sligo, Attracta left home to avoid the marriage arranged for her by her father, Talan, and she was received, along with a companion, into the religious life by St Patrick. As he blessed them, a veil fell from heaven which she reluctantly accepted. She founded a convent to which she later added a hospital in what is now Killraght near Boyle. Her feast day is 11 August.

B

Baithín (d. 598), first cousin of Colum Cille* and his immediate successor as abbot of Iona, was born in Donegal. They share the same feast day – according to tradition Baithín died on 9 June, the first anniversary of the Colum Cille's death.

Bee aka Bega (seventh century) was an Irish saint who founded a nunnery that survived for 900 years on a promontory in Cumbria which is still called St Bee's Head. The village of Killbees in Scotland also perpetuates her name. Bee preferred the religious life to the marriage planned by her father, an Irish king, and miraculously managed to slip away on the night before her wedding with the help of a bracelet given to her by an angel. After a period as a recluse on the Cumbrian coast, she was received as a religious by St Aidan* of Lindisfarne and encouraged by him to found her own establishment. Her feast day is 31 October.

Benen aka Benignus (d. *c.* 466) was the son of Sessenen and a convert to Christianity while still a child. According to tradition, he was the favourite disciple of St Patrick and his successor to the see of Armagh. In the legend of the Breastplate which St Patrick chanted on the way from Slane to Tara, the soldiers of Laoghaire, the high king, who were lying in wait, saw no men, only a herd of deer and one little fawn. Benen was the youngest one of the party and afterwards became known as the saint's psalm singer and later choirmaster. His name is perpetuated in Kilbennan, County Galway, where he founded a monastery. His feast day is 9 November.

Beoadh aka Beatus (d. 518–525) was originally Aeodh and had the prefix *Bo* added as a tribute to his saintliness. He was bishop of the early diocese of Ardcarne. His feast day is 8 March.

Bláth aka Flora (d. 523), the Latin form of the Irish for 'flower'. Bláth was a lay sister, working as the cook at St Brigid*'s convent in Kildare. She was was also known for her exemplary sanctity. Her feast day is 29 January.

Blathmac (d. 825) was of royal Irish blood, but he wanted to become a monk and, if possible, a martyr for the faith. He lived at the height of the Viking terror when Iona was left derelict and the Columban monks had brought their treasures to a new monastery at Kells. Blathmac and a companion reoccupied Iona, although the head of their order, Diarmait, stayed in Meath. When the Vikings attacked again in 825, Blathmac was slain on the steps of the monastic church. He was the subject of a verse biography by Walafrid of Strabo. His feast day is 15 January.

Boethian (fifth century) was born in Ireland and after studying with St Fursa*, he travelled to East Anglia and later to France with him. He established the abbey of Pierrepoint, near Laon in northern France, and was later murdered by local barons whom he had rebuked for their behaviour. His shrine is still a place of pilgrimage, especially on his feast day on 22 May.

Breaca (fifth-sixth century) was a disciple of St Brigid*. She went to Cornwall with a number of other sisters *c.* 460, landed in St Ives Bay and set up a convent on the east bank of the River Hayle. Her feast day is 4 June.

Brenach aka Brynach (?fifth century) was an Irish saint who settled in Wales and founded his establishment at the foot of a mountain called *Carn-Englyi* (Mountain of Angels) near Nefyn on the Lleyn peninsula in modern Gwynedd. The hill was so named because Brenach is said to have communed with angels on its top. His feast day is 7 April.

Brendan the Voyager aka Brandan (*c.* 486-578 or 583), the son of Findlugh, was born near Fenit, County Kerry and became in turn a pupil of St Ita*, St Finnian of Clonard*, St Enda*, St Jarlath* and St Gildas at Llancafarn near Cardiff. He founded several monasteries, including that of Ardfert near his birthplace and the great monastery of Clonfert in County Galway, which was noted for the austerity of its rule. His name is associated with a tenth-century account of marvellous voyages, *Navigatio Brendani*, in which he was said to have reached the American continent. According to the tale his companion monks fasted for forty days before setting out – calling at Aran to visit St Enda – and realising that an island where they found food and sheep was in fact the back of a whale. The 'land of plenty' that they finally reached has been identified variously as the Canary Islands and Florida. The saint undoubtedly did travel to Scotland and Wales and may indeed have made the epic seven-year journey that the *Navigatio* romanticises. He died at Annaghdown on Lough Corrib, at the convent founded by his sister St Briga. He is venerated as the patron saint of sailors and his feast day is on 16 May.

Brendan of Birr (d. 573) was a contemporary of St Brendan the Voyager* and a friend of Colum Cille*, who had a vision of his body being carried to heaven by angels. His foundation was at Parsonstown in County Offaly. His feast day is 29 November.

Brigid aka Bride (*c.* 450-*c.* 525), the premier Irish woman saint, is believed to have been born at Faughart, near Dundalk, County Louth, although some authorities suggest she came from County Offaly. She became a nun at a very young age and founded the double abbey of Kildare. Because of the Celtic worship of a deity called Brigit, a number of mythological tales associated with the goddess have been attributed to the saint, making it difficult to determine any reliable biographical facts. One legend tells of how she sat by the bed of a dying pagan chieftain, praying and plaiting rushes into a cross; when he enquired about the significance of the object, she explained and he asked to be baptised. The often elaborate rush crosses that are woven for her feast day on 1 February are associated with that legend but may actually originate from an earlier pagan rite of welcoming spring. The traditional image of Brigid is of a woman of great charity and joy in life. Her remains, like those of Colum Cille, were supposed to have been buried in St Patrick's grave in Downpatrick in order to prevent desecration by Vikings.

Bronach (sixth century), known as the Virgin of Glenshesk (in County Antrim), is also associated with the churchyard of Kilbroney near Rostrevor, County Down. The place was supposed to be haunted by the ringing of an invisible bell, and after a storm in 1885 a bell with a worn clapper was found in a fork of a fallen oak. It was identified as having a sixth-century design and is now revered as Bronach's Bell. She is the patron saint of seafarers and her feast day is 2 April.

Búite (d. 521) was the son of Bronach of the branch of Ciannachta who owned part of what is now County Louth. He journeyed to Rome and thence to Scotland, where he evangelised the Picts. He is said to have restored Nechtan, their king, to life and founded Kirkbuddo abbey. His great Irish foundation was Monasterboice in the Boyne Valley, which became a centre of learning as well as religious life. It was here that Flann Mainistreach (d. 1056) wrote verse histories of ancient and mythological Ireland. According to tradition, Colum Cille* was born on the day that Búite died. His feast day is 7 December.

Buriana (sixth century) was an Irish-born saint who, like Breaca*, left home to become a recluse in Cornwall. Her name is preserved in Buryan on the west coast of the peninsula, about five miles from Land's End. Her feast day is 4 June.

C

Cadroe (d. 976) was born in Scotland of Irish parents and educated in Armagh. He travelled to northern Europe by way of England, saving London from destruction by fire in the process. He became abbot of a new foundation at Waulsort on the Meuse in modern Belgium. He assumed charge of the dysfunctional monastery of St Clement in Metz *c.* 953 at the request of Bishop Adalbero. His feast day is 6 March.

Caimín (d. 653) was of royal blood, half-brother to Guaire Aidhne, king of Connacht. He was noted for his scholarship and the austerity of his life at his hermitage on Inis Cealtra in Lough Derg on the Shannon. A fragment of biblical commentary in his own hand is still extant. The foundation, known in later years as the Island of the Seven Churches, was frequently attacked by the Vikings as the Shannon provided a passage to the abbey door, but it survived until at least 1010. Caimín's feast day is 24 March.

Canice aka Cainneach, Kenneth (*c.* 525-*c.* 599), was a Pict, born in the Roe Valley of County Derry and educated by St Finnian* of Clonard and St Cadoc at Llancarfan near Cardiff. He worked for many years among the islands of the west coast and on the mainland of Scotland and acted, with St Comgall*, as guide and interpreter for Colum Cille* in his missions to the Picts. His name is preserved in several places, notably Inch Kenneth in Mull, and it is by that name he is still venerated in Scotland as a saint. He founded a church at what is now known as St Andrews in Fife. After returning to Ireland, he stayed for some time with his friend St Mobhi* of Glasnevin before founding the monastery of Aghaboe in County Laois, where he was buried. He remained the patron saint of the diocese of Ossory and has given his name to its capital, Kilkenny. His feast day is 11 October.

Cannera (d. 530) was a recluse living near Bantry in southwest Cork. Shortly before her death, she saw the church of St Senan* of Scattery Island (Inis Chathaigh) in the Shannon estuary and, deciding that it was the holiest place in Ireland, immediately made the difficult journey there. St Sennan would permit no woman near his church, but Cannera wrung from him the promise that he would give her extreme unction and allow her to be buried on the edge of the island. His insistence that the waves would wash her remains away had no effect, and the traditional site of her grave can still be seen. She is one of several patrons of boatmen, and her feast day is 28 January.

Carthage aka Cárthach Mochuda (d. 637) was born in the Sliabh Luachra region of Kerry and baptised, as the legend has it, in water from a fountain miraculously provided for the occasion. Like many others of his time, he spent a lot of his education journeying. He visited Comgall* of Bangor, Molua of Clonfert and Colmán Elo* of Lynally. His great foundation was Rahan in Offaly *c.* 590 for which he wrote the austere rule in verse. He was expelled from the foundation by King Blathmac at the urging of the monks of Durrow, however, probably because of his acceptance of the rulings of the Synod of Whitby (644). He made his way to Lismore, where another monastic school was established not

An illustration of St Kevin from a 12th-century manuscript
(Courtesy of the National Library of Ireland)

Beehive huts on the remote island-monastery of Sceilig Mhicíl,
off the coast of County Kerry (Bord Fáilte)

High Cross (*c.* ninth/tenth century) from St Columba's foundation at Durrow, County Offaly (Jacqueline O'Brien)

Beginning of St Patrick's Confession from the Book of Armagh (807 AD) (The Board of Trinity College Dublin)

The Arrest of Christ from the Book of Kells, written in a Columban monastery (*c.* 800 AD)
(The Board of Trinity College Dublin)

A representation of St Killian from the late-medieval period (Courtesy of the National Library of Ireland)

(Below)
Clonmacnoise, beside the River Shannon, County Offaly, where St Ciarán founded his monastery around 545 AD
(Jacqueline O'Brien)

long before his death. His feast day is 14 May.

Cathal aka Cathaldus (d. *c.* 681) was born in Munster and studied at, and eventually became master of, Lismore. He is said to have been asked to fill the vacant see of Taranto in southern Italy *c.* 666 on his way home from a pilgrimage to the Holy Land, and for the remainder of his life he served as its prelate. He is venerated still in Taranto, where his huge statue guards the port and a fresh water stream in the bay is known as *l'annello di san Cathaldo*, the ring of St Cathaldus, as it marks the place where he is believed to have stilled a storm by throwing his ring into the sea. He was the patron saint of the Italian army during World War I, and his feast day is 10 May.

Cellach aka Celsus (d. 1129) was born in Ulster and was a Benedictine monk at Glastonbury when he was ordained as the last hereditary archbishop of Armagh. He was noted for his reform of the whole Irish church and he was instrumental in securing the position of archbishop for St Malachy*, then the reluctant bishop of Connor. His last action as he lay dying was to send Malachy his crosier. His feast day is 1 April.

Ciarán of Clonmacnois aka Kieran (d. *c.* 516-549) was born in Connacht, the son of a carpenter, and educated by St Finnian* of Clonard and St Enda*. According to legend, he left home when still a young boy, driving a fine dun cow before him for sustenance. Destined for ecclesiastical greatness, he was led by visions to Clonmacnois, 'a quiet watered land, a land of roses' as Thomas William Rolleston put it in his poem 'The Dead at Clonmacnoise' on the Shannon *c.* 547. Clonmacnois became the greatest of all the monasteries/universities in Ireland. Ciarán did not survive long in his foundation – some say as little as seven months – but he left behind a notably austere rule and a tradition of piety, learning and fine art. His feast day is 9 September.

Ciarán of Saighir (d. *c.* 530) is known as the first-born of the saints of Ireland. He was from Clear Island and is said to have been sent back to Ireland by St Patrick* as his precursor after receiving religious training in Tours and Rome. He was one of the 'twelve apostles of Ireland' trained by St Finnian of Clonard. He founded the monastery of Saighir, near Birr in the territory of Ossory, of which he was the first bishop. He is the patron of the diocese and his feast day is 5 March.

Ciara (d. *c.* 680) was an Irishwoman directed into the religious life by St Fintan*. Her hermitage, which preserves her name, was at Kilkeary, near Nenagh, County Tipperary. Her feast day is 5 January.

Colmán of Lismore (d. *c.* 702) became abbot of Lismore in 689, and in his time it reached the height of its fame. His feast day is 23 January.

Colmán of Lindisfarne (d. 676) was born in Connacht and became a monk of Iona. He was chosen as the third bishop of Lindisfarne in 661 on the death of St Finan*. He is famous as an unrepentant supporter of the Celtic Church against the 'Romans', storming out of the council room at the Synod of Whitby in 664 and taking his monks with him to Ireland. He set up a monastery on Inishbofin off the Galway coast, but, due to a dissension between the English monks and the Irish, was forced to establish a separate house for his monks on the mainland in Mayo with an English abbot called Gerald. The region was known for long after as *Muigheó* *na Sacsan* (Mayo of the Saxons). Church politics aside, Colman was noted for his piety and the excellence of his rule at Holy Island at Lindisfarne. His feast day is 18 February.

Colmán of Armagh (fifth century) was a disciple of St Patrick*. He died during the apostle's lifetime and was buried by him. His feast day is 5 March.

Colmán of Dromore (sixth century) was probably born in Ulster and certainly established the abbey and bishopric of Dromore. He is said to have been the teacher of St Finnian of Clonard*. His feast day is 7 June.

Colmán Elo (555-610) was born in Tyrone, a nephew of St Colum Cille, and regularly visited the saint in Iona. He returned to Ireland on Colum Cille's death and founded the abbey of Muckamore near Antrim and became one of the patrons of the diocese of Down and Connor *c.* 590. He also established the important monastery of Lynally (Lann Elo) near Tullamore *c.* 600. His feast day is 26 September.

Colmán of Stockerau (d. 1012) was an Irish monk who was seized, tortured and hanged by local ruffians at Stockerau near Vienna while he was on pilgrimage to the Holy Land. His tomb at Melk was erected by the Holy Roman Emperor Henry II and, because of the miracles wrought by his relics, he became a patron saint of Austria. His feast day is 13 October.

Colmán of Kilmacduagh (c. 550–c. 632) was born in Kiltartan, County Galway, the son of the Irish chieftain Duac, and educated by St Enda* on Inishmore. He lived as a recluse in the Burren in County Clare until his meeting with King Guaire Aidhne of Connacht. Legend has it that the king's feast was whipped from before his eyes on Easter Sunday and when he and his train followed it they found Colmán, weak from his Lenten fast, happily tucking in. The king prevailed upon him to found a monastery in his territory and as they walked about, Colmán's girdle fell to the ground. He took this to be a sign and founded a great abbey at Kilmacduagh near Gort. His feast day is 29 October.

Colmán of Terryglass (d. 549) was a prince of Leinster and a fellow student of Colum Cille* at Clonard. He founded the monastery of Clonenagh at Mountrath in County Laois but preferred the solitude of Terryglass on the shore of Lough Derg in the Shannon. He died there of the plague. His feast day is 13 December.

Columban aka Columbanus (*c.* 540-615) was born in south Leinster and educated by Comgall* of Bangor, having been driven to the monastic life by the attentions of *lascivae puellae* (lecherous girls). He was noted for his austerity; the rules he devised for his houses in Europe were so extreme that they were eventually rejected after his death in favor of the more benign rule of St Benedict. At the age of forty-five, Columban obtained permission from Comgall to preach the Gospel in the barely Christian land of the Franks. He took with him an apostolic twelve companions, including St Gall* with whom he is said to have later quarrelled, and after much travail he established three houses at Annegray, Luxeuil and Fontaine in northeastern France. Uncompromising of temperament, he was often at odds with the local princelings and their consorts, and in 610 was expelled from his own monasteries. On one occasion, he was actually at sea and bound for Ireland from Nantes when his craft was blown back to the Breton shore. He went west to Metz and thence over the Alps into Switzerland, a harrowing journey for a man in his seventies, ancient by the standards of the times. It was here that the supposed quarrel with Gall occurred, and it was not settled until he was on his deathbed. He finally settled in Bobbio, south of Milan, accepting shelter from the Arian Duke Agilulf yet continuing to write and preach against the heresy. Columban was the greatest of all the Irish *peregrini*, the missionaries who left their homeland as exiles for Christ. He was witty, cultured and had a considerable poetic gift. His abrasiveness was rooted in the seriousness of his mission and may well have hidden an excessively tender nature. He died in Bobbio on 23 November, which is a feast of the universal Church.

Colum Cille (521-597), Ireland's 'first exile', was born in Gartan in central Donegal of aristocratic lineage – his father was Feidlimid of the Cenél Conaill family and his mother was Eithne, a princess of Leinster. He studied with St Mobhi* at Glasnevin, St Enda* in Aran and St Finnian* at Clonard. He was engaged in study, preaching, teaching and copying the Scriptures for seventeen adult years, and during his long life he founded monasteries at Swords, Durrow and Iona. He is patron saint of Derry, where his first foundation (546) is believed to have been. In 563 he left with the appropriate twelve companions to be, according to his biographer St Adamnán*, 'an exile for Christ' and lived in Iona for the rest of his life, apart from a few journeys home on specific, often political, business. The most important of these trips was to the great council of Drum Ceatt near Limavady, which had been called to settle dynastic questions for the kingdom of Dál Riata, which had territory in Ireland and Britain. The council also regularised the position of the *filid*, the learned laity, and earned for Colum Cille a number of verse tributes. He was the greatest of the native Irish saints and the subject of more wonder tales than any other of the *sancti*, even St Patrick*. His reasons for leaving the country have been ascribed to spleen and contrition for his involvement in a war between the northern Uí Néill family – of which the Cenél Conaill was a branch – and the *ard rí* (high king) Diarmait Mac Cerbaill. That war culminated in a ferocious battle near Ben Bulben and cost 3,000 lives. According to legend, the *ard rí* decreed that the psalter that Colum Cille had laboriously copied from that of St Finnian of Moville* belonged to the owner of the original text: 'to every cow its calf'. The real reason for Colum Cille leaving, however, was almost certainly *bán-martra* ('white martyrdom'), an exile notably painful for the homeloving Irish. The significance of his foundation in Iona cannot be exaggerated; it was the centre for the evangelisation of Scotland and Northumbria and remained an active Irish monastery until the thirteenth century in spite of savage Viking raids. As well as being the hero of many stories, Colum Cille is credited with much verse. He did write *Altus Prosator* and *Noli Pater* and other Latin verse. The *Cathach*, a Latin psalter and the oldest surviving text in Ireland, is said to be in his handwriting. His feast day is 9 June.

Comgall (*c.* 516-601) was born in Antrim of Pictish extraction and spent some time as a soldier. He was among the party that accompanied Colum Cille on the tour of Pictland which may have resulted in the conversion of King Brude in Inverness. On his return to

Ulster, he founded in 555 the great abbey of Bangor, County Down, which was noted for its dedication to learning and its austere rule. Among its alumni were St Columban*, St Gall*, St Moluag*, St Maelrubha* and St Malachy*. The *Antiphonary of Bangor,* created between 680 and 691, which contains a long hymn in praise of its founder, is the glory of Bangor just as the *Book of Kells* is the glory of Iona. Comgall died in Bangor and his feast day, as a patron of the Down and Connor diocese, is 10 May.

Conleth aka Conlaed (d. *c.* 519) was an associate of St Brigid*, spiritual director of her double abbey in Kildare and abbot-bishop of the monastery. Before joining her, he had been a hermit on the banks of the Liffey. In his earlier life, he was one of the chief artisans of Ireland and was famous for his metalwork and penmanship. His feast day is 4 May.

Corbinian (670-730) was of Irish birth and education and made a pilgrimage to Rome after fourteen years as a hermit. There he was ordained bishop by Gregory II and sent to help St Boniface with the task of evangelising Germany. He established his see at Freising in Bavaria.

His later years were made difficult by the local lord Duke Grimoald, whose incestuous marriage Corbinian had denounced. His feast day is 8 September.

Corbmac (sixth century) was a disciple of St Colum Cille and appointed by him as abbot of Durrow. His feast day is 21 June.

Cronán (d. 617) was born in the O'Carroll territory of Éile in Munster and educated at Clonmacnois. His first habitation was on a promontory of Lough Cré, which proved difficult to access for the poor and others who came to visit him, so he set another one up in what is now the site of the modern town of Roscrea. The seventh-century *Book of Dimma*, a copy of the Gospels thought to have been written by the scribe Dimma 'in forty days and forty nights without break' originated there. Cronán's feast day is 28 April.

Cummian Fada (592-662) was of the royal family of the Eoganacht and came from Killarney. He was in charge of the monastic school of Clonfert and later founder of a monastery at Kilcummin near Killala, County Mayo. He was noted for his energetic support of the 'Roman' church regulations promulgated at the Synod of Whitby in 664 over the Columban rules. Indeed, it was largely due to his writings that most of southern Ireland had already accepted the contentious Roman rules. His feast day is 12 November.

D

Davnet aka Damhnat (sixth century) founded a nunnery at Tydavnet (Davnet's House) near Monaghan. Her staff, the *Bachall Damhnait,* is in the National Museum. It was used for the testing of oaths and was believed to have had the power to permanently twist the mouths of liars. The rendering of her name as Dympna has led to the confusion of St Davnet with St Dympna of Gheel in Flanders, patron of the mentally ill, who is also said to have been of Irish origin. Davnet's feast day is 13 June.

Declan aka Deálgán (fifth century), a pre-Patrician saint, was born a prince of the Decies in Waterford and fostered with a Christian. He went to Rome to study, was consecrated bishop there and was later confirmed in his seat of Ardmore by St Patrick* himself. The area on the coast near Youghal harbour was once an island but, according to tradition, Declan attached it to the land (possibly with help from tide-silting). His monastery there was an important ecclesiastical centre for many years. The site still has the ruins of Declan's church and a magnificent round tower. Among many wonders ascribed to the saint are the raising of plague victims to life and the ending of the pestilence. In addition, he is reputed in old age to have sunk a fleet of marauding pirates. Declan's feast day is 24 July.

Diarmaid (sixth century) was the spiritual director and teacher of St Ciarán* of Clonmacnois. His feast day is 10 January.

Diarmaid (d. 823) founded a hermitage, Díseart Díarmada, at Castledermot, County Kildare in 818 which was the nucleus of an important early monastery. His feast day is 21 June.

Dichul aka Deicola (d. *c.* 625) was a monk of Bangor and a companion of St Columban* in his travels in Burgundy. He helped to found Luxeuil in northeastern France. When Columban was expelled by Queen Brunehaut, Dichul was too old to travel but stayed as a recluse in the Vosges, founding the abbey of Lutra. His feast day is 18 January.

Donatus (d. 874) was an Irishman who, on his return home from a pilgrimage to Rome in 829, stopped at Fiesole, the Etruscan town in the hills above modern Florence. His coming was seen as a sign as the see was vacant. He ruled as bishop until the year before his death and wrote a lot of poetry, including a verse life of St Brigid* and a description of his homeland. He established hospices for pilgrims throughout his diocese. His feast day is 22 October.

Donnán (d. 618) was a monk of Iona and founder of a monastery c. 600 on the island of Eigg, between Mull and Skye. He and his fifty-two monks were slain on Easter Sunday by 'sea-rovers', probably Scandinavian mercenaries hired by the local Pictish queen. The island Eilean Donan in Loch Alsh preserves his name. His feast day is 17 April.

Drostan (d. c. 610) was a monk of Iona and abbot of the monastery of Deer, in Aberdeen-shire, the last monastery thought to have been founded by Colum Cille. It survived as a Celtic monastery until the thirteenth century, when it became Cistercian. The saint has a holy well at Aberdour on the Firth of Forth. He is a patron of the Scottish church and his feast day is on 11 July.

Dunchadh (d. 717) was abbot of Iona from 710 until his death. It was in his time that the Roman customs promulgated at Whitby in 664, such as dating Easter, were finally accepted by the Columban foundations. His feast day is 25 May.

E

Eithne & Fidelma (fifth century) the shortest-lived saints of Ireland, were the daughters of Laoghaire, the high king of Tara. They chanced upon St Patrick as he journeyed from Slane to Croaghan, the residence of the kings of Connacht. Impressed by his saintly aura, they questioned him about his mission and were instructed in the faith. They were baptised where they knelt and immediately wished to become holy sisters. They asked to die soon so that, freed from the imprisonment of their bodies, they could behold the Lord. They died shortly after receiving communion from St Patrick. Their feast day is 11 January.

Enda (d. 530) was the father of Irish monasticism, having studied its principles at the famous *Candida Casa* school of monks at Galloway. He was of the Ciannachta, the same sect as St Búite*, and, like St Comgall*, had been a soldier.

He established his monastery on Inishmore, the largest of the Aran Islands, and it was noted more for its austerity than for the usual monastic occupations of study and copying. It was often used as place of retreat by other *sancti*. Enda died at his monastery at Killeany. His feast day is 21 March.

Erc (*c.* 512) was a learned member of the court of Laoghaire, high king of Tara, and was St Patrick*'s traditional adversary. He was the only one of those who confronted St Patrick on the hill of Slane, County Louth, on the first Christian Easter Sunday in Ireland, to give him homage. He was made a bishop by St Patrick and established his hermitage at Slane, where it grew and flourished as a monastic school. He is supposed to have been the tutor of Brendan* the Voyager. His feast day is 2 November.

Eugene aka Eoghan (sixth century) was born in Tyrone and studied with St Tigernach at Clones before both were captured by marauders and carried off to Britain as slaves. They were rescued but stayed to become monks at the great school of *Candida Casa* in Galloway. Eugene returned to Ireland and established the monastery of Kilnamanagh ('church of the monks') at Tallaght. His more famous foundation was at Ardstraw near Newtownstewart, County Tyrone. He was abbot-bishop of the Ardstraw diocese, which was later assigned to Derry, of which he is the diocesan patron. His feast day is 23 August.

Eusebius (d. 884) was an Irish pilgrim who became a Benedictine monk in the abbey of St Gall* in Switzerland. He obtained permission to live as an anchorite on Mount Saint Victor on the Vorarlberg in the Austrian Alps. He was killed by a scythe-wielding peasant whom he had chided for his godless ways and has since been revered as a martyr. His feast day is 31 January.

F

Fachanan (sixth century) was the first bishop of Ross. He founded a school at Rosscarbery in County Cork and St Brendan* the Voyager was one of his teachers. He is the patron of the diocese of Ross.

Fanchea (d. *c.* 520) was the daughter of a king of Oriel and sister of St Enda* of Aran. She founded a convent at Rossory, on the Lower Erne near Enniskillen. According to tradition, Enda helped Fanchea to build the house. She established a sister convent to her brother's foundation at Killeany on Inishmore and is buried there. Her feast day is 1 January.

Fergal aka Vergil (d. 784) was an Irish monk who trained at St Canice*'s monastery at Aghaboe. He left on a pilgrimage to the Holy Land *c.* 740 but remained in Bavaria to help St Rupert evangelise Austria. He was eventually placed in charge of the diocese of Salzburg but was too humble to accept ordination as bishop. He was an intellectual, known as the 'Geometer', and was twice reported to Rome by St Boniface for his views on such matters as the earth's structure. His work of evangelising Carinthia was thoroughly successful. His feast day is 27 November.

Fiachra (d. *c.* 670) was a hermit who went to France *c.* 650 and unwittingly named the four-wheeled cabs which were first seen in 1620 outside the Hôtel Saint-Fiacre in Paris. He is said to have administered the last rites to St Comgall* and to have set up hospices for male pilgrims when he was established as a hermit in Brieux. His reputation as a gardener and curer of syphilis made his shrine at Meaux a popular place of pilgrimage. His feast day is 30 August.

Finan (d. 661) was an Irish monk of Iona who succeeded St Aidan* as abbot of Holy Island at Lindisfarne and continued the work of evangelising Northumbria, baptising Peada, the son of the pagan King Penda, and Oswiu, who had killed both his Christian brother Oswin and Penda. He brought the faith to the lands south of the Humber, assisted by the English St Cedd. He was a strong opponent of the proposed

'Roman' changes that would bring the Columban practice in line with that of the Universal Church. He died three years before the Synod of Whitby which ruled against the Irish practice. His feast day is 17 February.

Findbar aka Finbar, Bairre (d. *c.* 633) was born at Rath Raithleann, near Crookstown, County Cork, of a Connacht father, a metalworker who moved to Munster to find work and married a slave girl. Findbar left home with three un-identified ascetics and spent much time in mission work in Scotland before establishing various hermitages in his native area, notably Kilclooney and on an island in Gougane Barra, which bears his name. Among many wonder tales associated with him is a story about him being led by an angel from the source of the Lee at Gougane Barra to its marshy mouth, where he founded his most important monastery and out of which grew the see and city of Cork. Findbar died at Cloyne and his remains were taken to Cork to be enclosed in a silver shrine. His feast day is 25 September.

Finnian of Clonard (d. *c.* 549) was, after St Enda*, the earliest of the founding fathers of

Irish monasticism and much more influential because of the convenient locations of his foundations. He was born at Myshall, County Carlow and educated at St Cadoc's monastery at Llancarfan, where he was a friend and fellow-pupil of St Gildas. At his great monastery of Clonard in County Westmeath he trained the 'twelve apostles of Ireland': Ciarán of Saighir*, Ciarán of Clonmacnois*, Brendan of Clonfert*, Brendan of Birr*, Colum Cille*, Colmán of Terryglass*, Molaise of Devenish*, Canice of Aghaboe*, Ruadhan of Lorrha*, Mobhi of Glasnevin*, Sinell of Cleenish* and Ninidh of Inishmacsaint. Like his master St Cadoc he emphasised the pre-eminence of study and urged his pupils to set up their own establishments. Although he was ascetic himself, his rule was milder than those of St Comgall* or St Enda*. He died of plague. His feast day is 12 December.

Finnian of Moville (*c.* 493-579) did his early training at the great school of monks at *Candida Casa* in Galloway. He was taken there by the abbot from his first school at Nendrum near Comber in County Down. He spent twenty years in Scotland as student and missionary, leaving, according to one story, because a Pictish girl had fallen in love with him. He visited Rome and obtained Latin copies of the Scriptures – the Vulgate – which he brought to Ulster in 540. For that reason his school at Moville, five miles from Bangor, in present day Newtownards, was the leading school of biblical study. Finnian's feast day is 10 September.

Fintan of Clonenagh (d. 603) was a disciple of Colum Cille*. During his abbacy of Colmán*'s at Clonenagh, it gained the reputation of being the most rigorously austere of all the houses in Ireland. The monks ate no meat and did not use animals to help with their farm work. The most luxurious food was vegetables and the abbot subsisted on stale barley bread and muddy water. In fact, the conditions were so bad that the monks in neighbouring houses objected. St Fintan's feast day is 17 February.

Fintan of Rheinau (d. 879) was born in Leinster. He was carried off as a slave to Orkney by Norse raiders but managed to escape to mainland Scotland. He undertook a pilgrimage to Rome in thanksgiving and became a Benedictine monk, spending his final twenty-two years as an anchorite at Rheinau, near Schaffhausen on the Rhine in Switzerland. His feast day is 15 November.

Flannan (seventh century) was a prince of the Dál gCais in modern County Clare. After much missionary work in the Hebrides, he was ordained bishop of his native diocese of Killaloe by Pope John IV in 640 and is its patron saint. He was famous for managing to recite the entire psalter each day in spite of all his labours. His feast day is 18 December.

Foillán (d. 655) was a brother of Fursa* and Ultan*. He travelled with them to East Anglia and helped found the monastery of Cnobheresburg in the ruins of Burgh Castle, near Yarmouth in Norfolk. When Fursa left for France, Foillán became abbot but had to leave because of attacks by the pagan Mercians. He established a monastery at Nivelles in Belgium to complement the nunnery founded there by Queen Itta, and he founded another house at Fosses. On a journey from one to the other, he was murdered by robbers in the forest of Seneffe. His feast day is 31 October.

Fridian (d. 588) was an Irishman who went on pilgrimage to Rome and decided to stay in order to found an Irish monastery on continental Europe. A doughty opponent of Arianism, he established a house at Lucca, twelve miles from Pisa, and became bishop in 560. He is credited with changing the course of the Auser, which was once a tributary of the Arno but now flows directly into the Ligurian Sea. His wax effigy, containing his relics, are in a glass coffin in the main church of Lucca. His feast day is 18 March.

Fursa aka Fursey (d. 648) was, after St Columban*, the best known of Irish missioners in Europe. He gained such a reputation as a preacher in Ireland that he decided, in the words of St Bede, 'to go on pilgrimage for the Lord wherever opportunity offered.' He and his brothers Foillán* and Ultan* came first to East Anglia after 630 and established the monastery of Cnobheresburg in the ruins of Burgh Castle, near Yarmouth in Norfolk. He stayed there for ten years before crossing to France and founding an abbey at Lagny, near Paris, in 644. The mayor Erchinoald became his patron and when Fursa died at Mézerolles on his way back to England, Erchinoald took the saint's uncorrupted body to be the centrepiece of the new cathedral at Péronne on the Somme, known thereafter as *Peronna Scottorum* (Peronne of the Irish). Fursa was famous for his ecstasies and visions of the spirit world, which were chronicled by St Bede and became the inspiration for Dante's *Divine Comedy*. His feast day is 16 January.

G

Gall (*c.* 550-645) was a student of St Columban* at Bangor and a useful companion on the mission to the land of the Franks because of his ability as a linguist. Towards the end of Columban's life in 612, he established a monastery at Bregenz on Lake Constance and stayed about a year, but on the death of his patron, who was killed by his pagan brother, he was anxious to move on over the Alps and perhaps reach Rome. According to the legend, Gall fell ill and refused to leave his lakeside hermitage, and Columban, irascible as ever, accused him of malingering. According to Gall's biographer, Walafrid of Strabo, Columban said to his faithful companion of many years, 'I enjoin on you before I go, that so long as I live in the body, you do not dare to celebrate Mass . . . ' Columban's abbatial staff arrived five years later, sent by the dying monk to release Gall from the interdict. Gall quickly learned the local language and began to convert the Alemanni, the local pagan tribe. He died at the age of about ninety-five, leaving a reputation for sanctity and austerity of life, and great skill as an angler. The monastery and town of Sankt Gallen, forty-five miles east of Zürich, were founded by the Benedictine monk Otmar in 712 and lasted until its suppression in 1797. It is famous for its library, which was begun by an Irishman, St Moengal*, c. 850. St Gall's feast day is 16 October.

Gobain (d. c. 670) was an Irish monk who accompanied St Fursa* to Burgh Castle and afterwards went with him to France. He was murdered at his hermitage fifteen miles west of Laon at the place now called Saint-Gobain, which is noted for its production of glass. His feast day is 20 June.

Gobnait (?sixth century) is thought to have been born in County Clare and to have lived in Inisheer, one of the Aran Islands, where there is a ruin called Kilgobnet. She was abbess of Ballyvourney, County Cork, placed there by its founder, St Abbán*. Among many legends associated with Gobnait is that she repelled a cattle raider by letting a swarm of bees loose on him. A much worn thirteenth-century wooden statue of the saint used to be displayed in the church at Ballyvourney on her feast day, which is on 11 February.

I

Ia aka Hia, Ives (d. 450) was an Irish nun who crossed to Cornwall as a missionary and was martyred at her cell at the mouth of the Hayle river. She left her name to the town of St Ives. Her feast day is 3 February.

Ibar (fifth century) was one of the pre-Patrician saints of Ireland and the last to yield to the apostle's authority. One story, which suggests that the basis for his opposition was that St Patrick was a foreigner, tells how when Patrick threatened to expel him, Ibar answered, 'Wherever I be I shall call it Ireland!' He founded his school on a island in Wexford harbour called Beggerin ('little Ireland'). His feast day is 23 April.

Ita aka Íde (*c*. 480-*c*. 570) was, after St Brigid, the most venerated female saint in Ireland, and like Brigid she is the subject of many wonder tales, including one which claims that she suckled the infant Jesus. The historical Ita – originally called Deirdre – was born in Drum, County Waterford of Christian parents. The name *Íde*, meaning 'hungry for God', was adopted. She established the nunnery that bears her name at Killeedy (*Cill Íde*) in County Limerick. Brendan the Voyager* was believed to have been one of her pupils. Her fame spread beyond Ireland; she featured in one of the poems of Alcuin (*c.* 737-804), Charlemagne's main cultural adviser. Her feast day is 15 January.

J

Jarlath aka Íarlaith (d. *c.* 550) was a disciple of St Benen* at Kilbennan County Galway and chose to stay close to his master when he founded his own monastery at Cluain Fois in Tuam, two-and-a-half miles away. He is patron of the archdiocese that originated there. His feast day is 6 June. An earlier St Jarlath became the third bishop of Armagh.

K

Kevin aka Coemgen (d. *c.* 618) was born in what is now County Wicklow and is said to have been the nephew of St Eugene*. He was educated by St Petroc of Cornwall, who was in Ireland at that time, and also by the monks of Kilnamanagh at Tallaght in County Dublin. He retired to a cell in Holywood near Blessington County Wicklow, but found it too worldly and retreated to the lonely but beautiful Glendalough. His wish for solitude was denied again as so many flocked to be near him, and reluctantly he founded a monastery with himself as abbot. He insisted on utter solitude during Lent. There are many stories associated with St Kevin, including his pursuit by a beautiful maiden, and of all the early saints, he was the one regarded as being most in tune with nature. The story of his holding, motionless, an egg laid by a blackbird in his hand until it hatched is typical. His feast day is 3 June.

Kilian (*c.* 640–*c.* 689), from Mullagh in County Cavan, preached Christianity to the Thuringians and Franconians. He travelled a lot, using Würzburg in Bavaria as his centre. One of his converts was Duke Gozbert, who had married Geilana, his dead brother's wife. Kilian declared the marriage invalid and he and two companions were later murdered, at her instigation. His body is buried in the crypt of the Würzburg cathedral that bears his name. His feast day is 8 July.

L

Laserian aka Laisren, Molaise (d. 639) was trained at *Candida Casa* in Galloway, the great school of monks. He was the founder of the monastery and the ancient diocese of Leighlin in County Carlow. He travelled to Rome and was appointed by Pope Honorius I as apostolic delegate, acting as troubleshooter in the great controversy over divergences in Roman and Celtic church practices, which were finally settled at the Synod of Whitby in 664. He is also believed to be the founder of Teampall Mo-Laisse on Inishmurray, off the Sligo coast. His feast day is 18 April.

Laurence O'Toole aka Lorcán Ó Tuathail (1128-1180) was born in Leinster and was for a period of his childhood kept hostage by Diarmait Mac Murchadha, who brought the Normans to Ireland. At the age of twelve, he became an Augustinian canon at Glendalough and abbot at twenty-six. Eight years later he was made Archbishop of Dublin and the delegate to treat with Richard le Clare ('Strongbow') when the Normans attacked the city in 1170. Realising that the invaders were stronger than any opposition the warring Irish could muster, he submitted to Henry II, who came with a large army and papal authority in the shape of the disputed *Laudabiliter* in 1172. He remained as go-between of the Irish and the English, a task made almost impossible by the personalities of Ruairí Ó Conchúir, the high king, and Henry. He was only reluctantly granted permission to travel across England on his way to take part in the Third Lateran Council in Rome in 1179. Then Henry refused him permission to return to Ireland, and the saint died at Eu in Normandy, where he had followed the king hoping to make him change his mind. He was canonised in 1226, and his feast day is 14 November.

Lurach (sixth century) was born of royal blood in south Derry and founded the monastery of Maghera, County Derry, which bears his name (*Machaire Rátha Luraigh*). It was the seat of the diocese after Ardstraw was downgraded. His feast day is 17 February.

M

Macartan (d. 505) was an early disciple of St Patrick* and is said to have been his bodyguard. St Patrick* ordained him as abbot-bishop of the see of Clogher, which stretched from the Irish Sea to Donegal Bay and takes in much of southwest Tyrone. He is the patron saint of the diocese. His feast day is 24 March.

Macdara (fifth century) gave his name to an island off Carna County Galway when he founded a monastery there. Until recent times local boats dipped their sails three times when passing it. There used to be pilgrimages there on 16 July and 25 September, both taken to be the saint's feast days.

Catherine McAuley (1778-1841), the founder of the order of the Sisters of Mercy, was born in Stormanstown House, Ballymun and brought up by a Quaker couple, the Callahans of Coolock House, after her father's early death. She became a rich woman on her guardians' death in 1822 and decided to use her wealth to relieve the appalling state of the Dublin poor. With some women friends she set up a 'house of mercy' in Baggot Street but soon found her attempts at alleviating the urban misery blocked by clerical obduracy. With great reluctance she and her companions – who would have preferred to remain members of the laity – constituted themselves as a religious order in 1835; it was finally approved by Gregory XVI in 1841, five months before the founder's death. By then there were ten convents in Ireland and two in England. Mercy Sisters made up half of Florence Nightingale's band of nurses at Scutari during the Crimean War and with 23,000 sisters worldwide, the order is now the largest congregation of women in the Church. The process for the canonisation of this reluctant nun is well advanced.

Maelruain (d. 792) may very well, as his name suggests, have been a disciple of St Ruadhan* of Lorrha. He was founder of the monastery of Tallaght County Dublin *c.* 755, and his austere rule made him the obvious leader of the Céle Dé ('the serving companions of God') or Culdee movement that reformed the Irish monastic system in the eighth and ninth centuries. His feast day is 7 July.

Maelrubha (d. 724) was a member of St Comgall*'s community at Bangor. He left for Iona and spent nearly fifty years (673-722) as a roving missionary in northern Pictland. He founded the monastery of Applecross, in Ross, near Skye. His name is remembered in Loch Maree. His feast day is 21 April.

Malachy aka Mael, Maedoc (1095-1148), the reforming Archbishop of Armagh, was one of the very few incumbents to have been born in the see. His parents died when he was young and he was nurtured by a hermit called Eimar. Ordained at twenty-five by St Cellach*, he was given the task of reviving the abbey at Bangor in 1123 and the neglected diocese of Connor the following year. He pursued both tasks with vigour. He lived the ascetic life of a monk of Bangor until a hostile Ulster chief drove him and his monks out to seek peace and seclusion in Kerry in 1127. His appointment to the primatial see in 1132 plunged him into local politics once again. Cellach was determined to be the last hereditary archbishop, and his relatives opposed Malachy, putting his life in danger several times and retaining the diocese's treasure, including St Patrick's staff and the priceless Book of Armagh. Having wrought the necessary reforms, Malachy resigned the position to the abbot of Derry and returned to Connor, setting up an Augustinian foundation at Downpatrick. His greatest achievements were the reconciliation of the Celtic church with Rome, the establishment of canonical hours and the revival of the administration of the sacraments which had fallen into disuse. Formal papal recognition could come only with the presentation of *pallia*, lambswool collars which would mark authority, so Malachy went to Rome to seek them for Armagh and Cashel. On the way he stopped with St Bernard (1090-1153), the founder of the Cistercian order, at Clairvaux. The two men became friends and after Malachy's death, Bernard wrote his biography. Innocent II decreed that the *pallia* would be conferred only at the request of a national synod but made the saint his legate. Malachy returned home, bringing with him enough monks to establish the first

Cistercian abbey at Mellifont, and hastily summoned a synod at Inispatric near Skerries (1148). He was despatched again by the synod to Rome to bring home the *pallia* but died at Clairvaux on the way. Bernard buried him in his own habit and wore Malachy's for the remaining five years of his life. Malachy was canonised in 1190. His feast day is 3 November.

Marianus Scottus (of Cologne) aka Máel Brigte (1028-83) became a monk of Moville in Strangford Lough in 1052 and four years later he was sent into exile by the abbot Tighernach Bairrcec for a reason now unknown. He went to Cologne and stayed as a Benedictine monk in St Martin's abbey until 1058 when he was ordained at Fulda in central Germany and then had himself immediately immured. In 1069 he moved to a similar condition in the monastery of St Martin at Mainz, where he died. He was the author of the *Chronicon Universale*, which tells the story of the world from the Creation to 1082 and contains a lot of useful information about Irish ecclesiastical history, especially about the Irish in Germany. His feast day is 22 December.

Marianus Scottus (of Ratisbon) aka Muiredach Macc Robartaig (d. 1088) was born to a noble family in Donegal. In 1067 he went on a leisurely pilgrimage to Rome and was induced to become a monk while staying at the Benedictine abbey of Ratisbon (now Regensburg on the Danube, about sixty-three miles northeast of Munich). In 1078 he founded there the abbey of Weih Sankt Peter, thus originating the group of *Schottenklöster* (Irish monasteries) that lasted for several centuries in southern Germany. His feast day is 9 February.

Maugille aka Madelgisil (d. *c.* 655) was a companion and confidant of St Fursa* in his travels to England and France. He was Fursa's prior at Lagny near Paris and after his death in 648 became a monk at St Riquier near Centule. After a few years he retired to solitude at Monstrelet where he died. His feast day is 30 May.

Mel (d. *c.* 490) was a contemporary of St Patrick*, who made him bishop of Ardagh with a 'cathedral' near Mostrim in County Longford. The saint's staff is now in St Mel's Diocesan Museum in Longford. One significant story concerns his supposed error during the profession of St Brigid* when he made her a bishop and insisted that the conferring should stand. His feast day is 6 February.

Mobhi (d. *c.* 545) was one of the 'twelve apostles of Ireland' trained by St Finnian of Clonard*. Encouraged by his master, Mobhi set up his own monastic school at Glasnevin on the banks of the Tolka River in north Dublin. His was a kind of graduate school for other teachers and among his pupils were Colum Cille*, Comgall*, Ciarán* and Canice*. He died of the mid-sixth-century plague and his foundation did not survive his death. His feast day is 12 October.

Moengal aka Marcellus (d. *c.* 869), a disciple of St Gall*, was placed in charge of the cloister schools at Bangor. His best-known pupil was Notker Balbulus (*c.* 840-912) composer of church music and compiler of a *Martyrology* (891-6) which contained much information about Irish saints. Moengal was also noted for his interest in church music and for the excellence of his calligraphy. In the *Necrology* of St Gall, Moengal's death is recorded (in Latin) as that of 'the best and most learned of men' and in the *Annals of*

Ulster it is recorded for the year 871 that, 'Moengal the pilgrim, abbot of Bangor, brought his old age to a happy close.' His feast day is 27 September.

Molaise of Devenish (d. 564 or 571) suffers biographically from the fact that there are sixteen saints called Molaisse. He was one of St Finnian* of Clonard's 'twelve apostles of Ireland,' who were instructed by their master to set up their own hermitages. Molaise chose the tiny Devenish, an island in Lower Lough Erne, three miles from Enniskillen where he continued his friendship with Colum Cille*. He is believed to have made the arduous journey to Rome and to have brought back relics. The monastery that he founded used to hold the Soiscél Molaise, a book shrine now housed in the National Museum. His feast day is 12 September.

Moling (d. 697) was born in Wexford and studied at Glendalough. His first foundation was TechMoling in County Carlow which continued over the centuries, as St Mullins, to be one of the most important foundations of south Leinster. His name is also to be found in Timolin in County Kildare and in Tigh Moling near Inishtioge in County Kilkenny. Among many tales associated with the saint are that he could walk on water and that he introduced rye to Ireland. He became bishop of Ferns and was buried at St Mullins. His feast day is 17 June.

Moluag (*c.* 592) was a Pict from Dál Riata who studied at Bangor and established a monastery at Mortlach on the shores of Loch Linne in Argyll. He died at Rossmarkie. His feast day is 25 June.

Munchin (?seventh century) was of noble birth in Thomond and became abbot of the monastery at Mungret on the Shannon, which, according to tradition, was founded by Neassán a deacon who was a disciple of St Patrick*. He is the patron of the see of Limerick and his feast day is 2 January.

P

Patrick (*c.* 390-?461) the 'apostle of Ireland' was a Romano-Briton who was captured by Irish raiders at age sixteen and shipped to Ireland. After six years of slavery he became a student in Continental monasteries and a disciple of St Germanus (*c.* 378-448) at Auxerre. He was ordained bishop in France sometime before 432, when he left to establish the Catholic faith in the Ireland that he had grown to love. Although there were pockets of Christianity in the island before St Patrick's arrival, it was his work that essentially made the whole island Christian and laid the basis for its permanence. He travelled widely in Ulster, Leinster and Connacht preaching, baptising, opening monasteries and schools, and winning a majority of the Irish chieftains and their followers over to his side. He established Armagh as his primatial see (*c.* 444) but the pattern of Irish Church rule was to be abbatial rather than episcopal and diocesan. Uniquely among the *sancti* of the period, he has left two personal documents, *Confessio* and *Epistola ad Milites Corotici,* which depict a man full of humility, stern piety and righteous anger against the soldiers of a so-called Christian prince who killed Irish captives. According to tradition, he is buried in Downpatrick not far from the supposed site of his first church at Saul, County Down. His feast day is 17 March.

Pelligrinus aka Peregrinus (d. 634) was, as his name implies, an Irish pilgrim who on his return from the Holy Land established himself as a hermit in Modena, between Parma and Bologna. His feast day is 1 August.

Oliver Plunkett (1629-81) was born in Loughcrew, County Meath and ordained for the priesthood in Rome in 1654. He remained as professor of Theology at the college *de Propaganda Fidei* until 1669, when he was ordained Archbishop of Armagh. He was welcomed by his fellow Old English Catholics of the Pale but viewed with suspicion by the Gaelic clergy of the greater part of the archdiocese. The post-Cromwellian church was in need of reform and

Plunkett was full of Tridentine fervour. His work of reform was possible, albeit difficult, until the anti-Catholic frenzy that shook Britain after the fictitious 'Popish Plot' (1678) concocted by Titus Oates (1649-1705) caused the Dublin authorities to arrest the Archbishop of Dublin while Plunkett went into hiding. He was arrested in 1679 on trumped-up charges and executed at Tyburn. He was the last Catholic to be martyred in England. His disembowelled, quartered body lies in Downside Abbey and his head is preserved in St Peter's Church in Drogheda. He was canonised in 1975 – the latest Irish saint to be so honoured – and his feast day is 1 July.

R

Ronan (d. 664) was the most famous abbot of Dromiskin, which was founded by St Patrick* near Castlebellingham, County Louth. He appears in the story of Suibne Geilt, the king driven mad by the noise of the battle of Mogh Rath (Moira, County Down), as the cleric who cursed him. The madness consists of Suibne's thinking that he is a bird and the twelfth-century text describes his wanderings about Ireland until he finds peace at last in St Mullins, the abbey of St Moling*. The saint's relics were placed in a shrine in 801, but it disappeared during the Viking occupation in the tenth century. The name is also found in Kilronan, on Inishmore, on of the Aran Islands. His feast day is 18 November.

Ruadhan (d. 584) was one of the 'twelve apostles of Ireland' trained and sent forth by St Finnian* of Clonard. His foundation was at Lorrha in County Tipperary, eight miles west of Birr. It became one of the foremost abbeys in Munster boasting a miraculous food-giving tree and a scriptorium which produced the Stowe missal. St Ruadhan's bell is in the British Museum. His feast day is 15 April.

S

Senan (d. *c.* 540) was born in Kilrush in County Clare of rich parents who, legend says, had the religious life suggested to him when the waters of the Shannon estuary parted to allow him walk across. He was educated at Kilmanagh, near Callan in County Kilkenny. He established a monastery at Enniscorthy, County Wexford, before making a pilgrimage to Rome. On his way home he visited St David at Menevia. His great foundation was on Scattery Island (Inis Chathaigh) near Kilrush, and its stones since are said to be potent against shipwreck. His feast day is 8 March.

Sinell aka Sillan (sixth century) was one of the 'twelve apostles of Ireland' who studied with St Finnian* of Clonard and learned austerity. Following St Finnian's instructions to all his neophytes, Sinell established his own monastery at Cleenish, a tiny island in the many-islanded

Upper Lough Erne. The foundation was noted for the extreme severity of its rule, which rivalled that of St Fintan*'s at Clonenagh, and it was associated with St Comgall*'s Bangor. St Comgall's greatest alumnus, St Columban, spent his years as a novice at Cleenish. Sinell may have succeeded Comgall as abbot of Bangor. His feast day is 12 November.

T

Matt Talbot (1856-1925) was born in Dublin and worked for many years as a builder's labourer. He was an alcoholic in his younger years but took the pledge of abstinence in 1884 and spent the rest of his life in prayer, fasting and secret self-mortification, including wearing chains about his body. This regimen was not discovered until his sudden death in Granby Lane, near Dominick Street. He was declared 'Venerable' in October 1976, and the process for his canonisation continues.

Tassach (d. ?495) was an early disciple of St Patrick*, who placed the church at Raholp, near Downpatrick, into his care. An extant ruin is one of the oldest in Ireland. Tassach was an artificer, making church bells, crosses, chalices and monstrances. He is said to have administered the last rites to St Patrick. His feast day is 14 April.